Menagerie of Poems

Laura Couch

BookLeaf Publishing

Presentation by *BookLeaf Publishing*

Web: www.bookleafpub.com

E-mail: info@bookleafpub.com

ISBN: 978-93-95890-43-4

First edition 2022

DEDICATION

To all of us who slog through the mud of life to cry, laugh and learn grace along the journey. It's okay to rest, to fall, to get hurt,to take a break, to lean on someone, and to hold someone who needs strength.

ACKNOWLEDGEMENT

For all of those who see the world as a mysterious playground to be respected and explored, and the Earth's inhabitants as stewards of the vast ethereal beauty.

PREFACE

Suffering is temporary but I'm generally of the opinion, suffering is no picnic. Joy; pure joy, belly laughs and a childlike wonder are my saving grace.

Thief

Shrinking,
Ducking,
Eyes averted
Hammers, hammers, hammers
The words you shout are hammers.
The spit flies in my face,
Pounding the table with your fist
Finger pointed in my face.
Hammers, hammers,hammers
The words you shout are hammers...
Growing until the air is filled.
Constricting,
Creating the space between you and I.
Stealthily as a thief
Like A Death, final and swift
Robbing joy
Erasing dignity
Eroding love
Like A Death, final and swift.

Air

Flooded mind
Breath, breathe, breather,
Fleeting calm,
Breaking the surface of the water,
Saturated,
Sinking under from the weight of the hidden.
Bobbing up,
Gasping for air,
Ragged breathing,
Sobbing, rocking back and forth.
Flooded mind,
flooded.
Breath, in and out,
Counting, slowing,
Slowly Centering as a whirling dervish,
Spinning,
Full stop.
Watching as it floats
Returning to self,
Home.
Placing the thoughts
Neatly, in a row,
Categorized, alphabetized,
Shelved away.
Breathing in and out

I smile,
A wistful, lopsided half smile
But a triumph all the same.

Birth

Shaking, crying, pushing
As my bones separate
Retreating into a quiet corner of my mind
Feeling pain, an inexplicable intensity of pain.
Pause.
A sigh.
A lull, a peace, a window of rest
And a surge of energy takes over.
I become the energy.
I wail as you leave your dwelling place and
emerge.
A baby's cry breaks the hushed silence.
I feel an energy, a vibration, a relief, an endless
amount of love
flowing through me and in me.

Seesaw

How can I hop off this seesaw?
You laugh as my legs dangle,
As I grip on while suspended in the air,
As your weight roots you firmly to the Earth,
As you gain strength from my precarious
position.
As you laugh at my predicament.
Please may I come down? I ask
You laugh as my face crumples, my shoulders
sag,
You taunt me but say you are only joking.
My face goes blank.
 I hide my fear.
I rely on your weight to safely let me down.
 I hide my fear.
You are furious.
Quickly you hop off the seesaw, I am let down
with a bang.
A jolt.
A shock.
Back to the ground, I am rattled.
How can I hop off this seesaw?

Bitterness

Bitterness,
Choking vines grow underneath the surface
Unseen vines
Spread,
Grow,
Shoot up,
Leafy spread covering trees, ground,
Bleached gray barns.
Suffocating life,
stealing the sun,
Silently encroaching
Ever prolific
Until, hacking away at all the roots
And burning the rest
The suffocation halts
New life unfurls,
 full of sweetness and light,
Full of hope and promises.

Jester

See the worn shoes
With the bells on the toes,
And the faded smile.
The jester
Juggling jesting joking
Smiling all the while.
And as the night wanes
And the footsteps fade
The jester
Calmly puts away the smile
In a drawer for another day.

Shifting shapes

Why do I recoil at your voice
Why do I stiffen at your touch
Why did you decorate my skin with bruises?
No! Please stop!
Stop!
You're hurting me!
I plead.
Is this a game where you shake a leather bag,
spill the dice,
Decide,
 it is a five and one
So tonight,Is it tenderness but tomorrow is
screaming and grabbing?
Seems as arbitrary as the roll of a dice.
I stop struggling to break free of your grasp.
Later, you remark
I could tell when you got into it
And really started enjoying it.
Why do I recoil at your voice?
Why are you such a shape shifter?
My saying No! Is a right.
Your duty is to honor my
Intrinsic worth by respecting my right to say
Stop! No!

Strength

One cord can snap,
Fray,
Unravel.
Two cords intertwined can strengthen,
Bolster,
Hold fast,
Withstand the salt, the sun ,
the pounding surf.
I am a force to be reckoned with.
I am a strong, tenacious person
I am searching for a wingman,
arms to envelope me,
fingers to smooth my furrowed brow.
The second cord dwells within me.
I await my love, a whole person waiting to meet
my love

Where Two Souls Meet

I wait for my lover to return
False starts, another car passes by.
Finally you arrive and I want you,
My spirit yearns to be close to you, to meld into
you as we forge together and become stronger.
Salty, sweaty skin pressed into mine.
Feverishly our bodies tangle and untangle,
A cacophony of long legs and arms,
Fingers entwined, palms together,
Rising and falling, circular breathing,
Smelling your skin,
Rubbing my face lightly on your scratchy face,
Your face shimmering with fiery reds, glowing
tawny and ruddy.
Touching the soft, soft place where your beard
ends and your lip begins.
Marveling at your strength, thinking to myself,
You have my heart, as I surrender my body to
you.
Offering myself up to you, unabashedly holding
up a piece of fruit to share.
Take me, enjoy, here's some more of what you
love, like it? So deeply satisfying.
Our rhythm is slow, shuddering to a halt as our
bodies quiet and our minds still.

Our oneness is suspended in time,
This interlude and beauty the sacred space where
two souls meet,
Rocking back and forth,
Back and forth,
Sighing deeply,
deeply in love,
so very deeply in love

Joie de Vivre

Shrinking
Invisible
Like Alice in Wonderland,
Except without the Wonderful.
I shrink smaller and smaller.
I tuck my head down upon my chest and cower.
Why?
Am I a prize fighter past my prime?
A worn-out salesman in a wrinkled suit?
Where's my chutzpah?
My spark?
My stubborn streak?
I am faded like the wash on the line,
All my colors indistinct and blurry,
Faded blues, muted reds, all washed out, no
brilliance here.
Turning deep within, I find it,
Buried,but nonetheless here.
My soul, my radiance, my ear to ear grin, my
joie de vivre -
my dance.
Dancing to the rhythm of life like a whirling
dervish,
Hypnotically whirling,
Point and counterpoint.

Stopping and breathless,
Laughing out loud,
Head thrown back ,arms open,
My eyes fixed upon the stars--
This, This is
Who I Am.

Do I? I do, but, do you?

Watching the clothes spin,
I want to contort my body into the washer,
Spinning clean all my dull, achy, dirty
everydayness.
Why is the repetitiveness of life so enveloping,
shrouding me,
Dulling my thoughts?
Why do I work at
The washer,
The stove,
The sink,
The dishwasher?
 Have I worn a path in the linoleum from the
repetition?
Have I grown accustomed to the silence,
the loneliness,
the singular-ness of my life?
I suppose the loneliness transforms,
Blossoms into...
Into what?
The freedom of be-ing,
Despite the joys and trappings of my babies.
What does it mean, the bonds of matrimony?
Does it mean dissolving?

Does your solubility factor shoot way up upon
marriage?
Is it as if a chemical reaction takes place, the
bond of marriage equals solubility of the
individuals partaking in the bond.

Dancing in the Dark

Kissing babies,
 shaking hands,
 every person here
 is charmed by your brilliant smile so bright and
wide,
showing your sharp, sharp teeth.
Better to eat you with,my dear.
Returning home,
your 40-watt smile
Transforms into a scowl
 as you shift into your worn out chair
 All Words Cease.
 Robotically staring at the television.
 I pause to pose a question, but seeing the blank
stare,
 I know the heavy velvet curtain is drawn.
The show is over....
Until late into the night, when I am beyond
exhausted from singularly bathing, inventing
stories and putting to bed the kids,
You climb on top of me,
Grunting and thrusting until you
Moan, roll off me,
Start to snore
And I am left
Pondering the ceiling

In the dark.

Peripheral

I exist in the realm of your peripheral vision.
You see me but you do not see Me.
You tell me who I am.
What am I to you?
I am those things to you,
And it is utterly terrifying to ponder
Who you say I am as I exist
Peripherally in your mind.

Interrupted

Reading while nursing my babe and cajoling my
toddler to sleep,
A deep sadness is stirred within my
consciousness.
It is as if a scab on a wound I didn't know
existed was pulled off,
Which created an open wound that throbs and
stings.
It is funny, raw, clever and real.
Everything resonates within me.
I see myself... Interrupted.

Queen Bee

Sweetness,
golden, sticky sweetness.
You catch more flies with honey than vinegar, I
say.
I often wonder how it has come to be some
people I encounter are so wounded,
They snap at anything that moves near them.
I contemplate this, and while I sympathize,
My body tells me to stay away from those who
snap at me at the slightest provocation.
I want to wrap my arms around you,
my heart grows light when you're around.
I feel butterflies, jittery and
At peace when I'm in your presence.
When I'm with you
it is honey everywhere I look, dripping from the
honeycombs.

Pivot

Hysteria
Hysterical female
Listeria
Salmonella
Melodramatic female
Words have power
Choose them wisely
As they have intrinsic value and deep rooted
meaning.
Choosing to equate a powerful,strong and
capable woman
With anything other than a badass,
Is simply and unequivocally a misguided
misjudgment.
Remember that and pivot.
Bending in the storm allows us to survive with
resiliency.
Pivot.

Beacon

Cheeks flushed,
Heart racing
Keeping composure.
Does he notice how I stare?
I look away but stare again because I am
Mesmerized.
How were you here the entire time
Yet I looked past you
Due to being weighed down
By all the words from my previous lover.
Strength is gained from
Cutting the rope to drop the weighty net.
Shedding the weight,
I wonder how I carried it so long,
And let it slip silently into the deep dark depths
of the ocean.
Floating weightlessly on my back,
I flip over and start to swim towards you,
As you beam a smile and beckon with a wave.
You become my beacon,
And I yours.

Headstones

What will be said about me when I'm dead and
buried?
She tried?
Perhaps I would prefer the murmurings at the
funeral home to consist of this:
She was the kindest person I know.
She was a loyal and true friend.
She was a loving, doting mother.
She was fierce.
As I amble about this cemetery,
I pause and ponder,
What am I leaving behind?
The love I gave multiplied with each birth, and
my cup runneth over with love. Love is infused
in my life, and I am deeply filled with a
profound sense of gratitude.

www.ingramcontent.com/pod-product-compliance
Lightning Source LLC
Chambersburg PA
CBHW060927130726
48001CB00006B/2461